AFC BOURNEMOUTH

THE OFFICIAL
AFC BOURNEMOUTH
ANNUAL 2025

Written by Andrew Haines, Dan Rose,
Matt Joyce, Neil Perrett & Zoe Rundle

Designed by Lucy Boyd

g

A Grange Publication

© 2024. Published by Grange Communications Ltd.,
Edinburgh, under license from AFC Bournemouth.
Printed in the EU.

Photographs © Robin Jones, Amy Maidment,
Getty Images.

ISBN 978-1-915879-78-3

CONTENTS

Premier League Squad 2024/25   6

The Path to the Points Record   8

A Day in the Life: Malachi Ogunleye   16

Colour Me In   18

International Cherries   20

Marcus Tavernier: Question Corner   24

A Day in the Life: Toure Williams   26

125 for 125   28

Bourne in the USA   38

Colour Me In   40

A Day in the Life: Helen Bleazard   42

Iraola In Numbers   44

Ten Years on with Tommy   46

Invincible Cherries   50

A Day in the Life: Antoine Semenyo   52

Let's Get Quizzing!   54

Quiz Answers   62

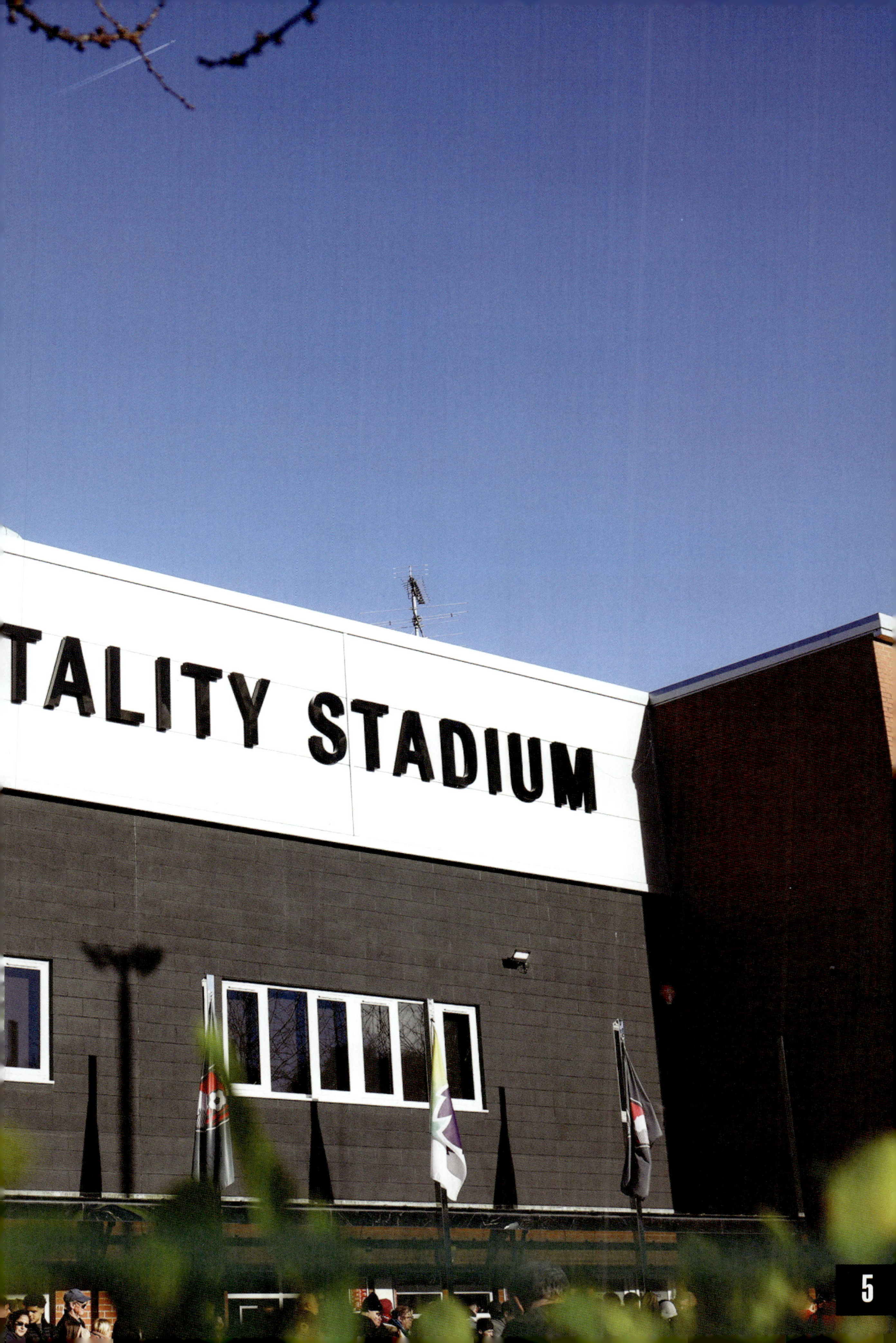
TALITY STADIUM

2024/25
PREMIER LEAGUE SQUAD

2. Dean Huijsen

3. Milos Kerkez

4. Lewis Cook

5. Marcos Senesi

7. David Brooks

8. Alex Scott

9. Evanilson

10. Ryan Christie

11. Dango Ouattara

12. Tyler Adams

13. Kepa Arrizabalaga (GK)

15. Adam Smith

16. Marcus Tavernier

17. Luis Sinisterra

19. Justin Kluivert

22. Julián Araujo

23. James Hill

24. Antoine Semenyo

26. Enes Ünal

27. Illia Zabarnyi

29. Philip Billing

35. Owen Bevan

37. Max Aarons

40. Will Dennis (GK)

42. Mark Travers (GK)

46. Callan McKenna (GK)

48. Max Kinsey

THE PATH TO THE
POINTS RECORD

The 2023/24 season was a truly historic and record-breaking campaign for AFC Bournemouth. With Andoni Iraola in his first year as head coach of the club, the team achieved the club's highest-ever total of 48 points in the Premier League. Here are the key moments of the route to the Cherries sealing a top-flight record...

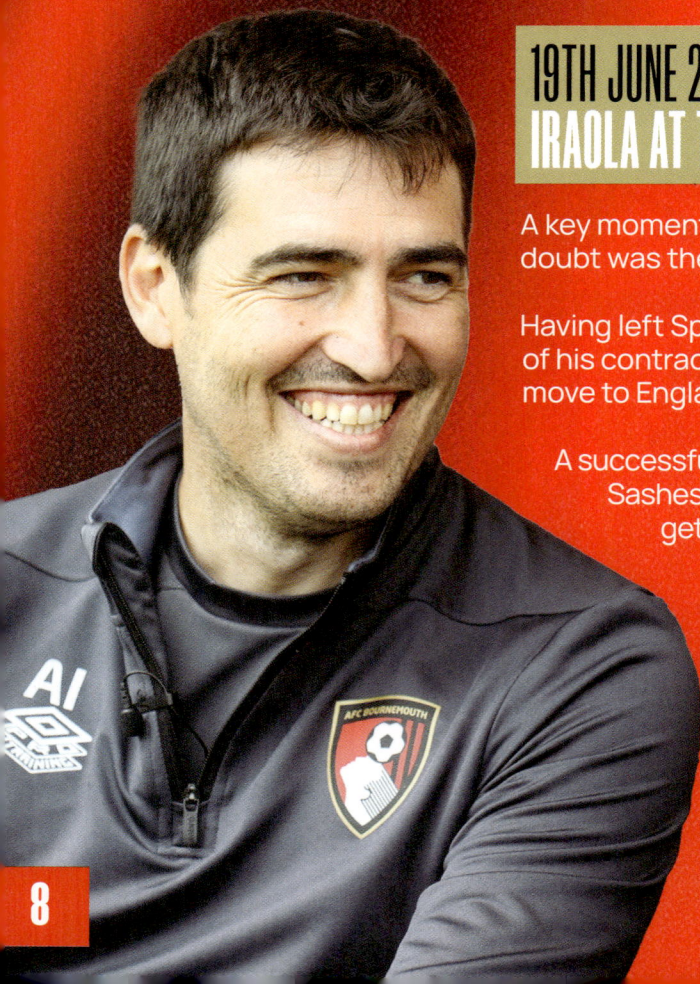

19TH JUNE 2023
IRAOLA AT THE WHEEL (0 PTS)

A key moment in the path to the points total without a doubt was the arrival of Andoni Iraola!

Having left Spanish club Rayo Vallecano upon the expiry of his contract with the La Liga outfit, the boss made the move to England.

A successful three-year spell with Los Franjirrojos (the Red Sashes) had left Iraola in demand, with the Cherries getting themselves to the front of the queue.

Upon arrival in Bournemouth, he put pen to paper on a two-year deal at Vitality Stadium.

With pre-season getting underway soon after, the head coach quickly got to work on planning his first season in English football.

AFC Bournemouth owner and chairman Bill Foley's thoughts at the time: "We're so excited to welcome Andoni to the club.

"With his contract in Spain coming to an end this summer, we wanted to act quickly.

"He was highly sought after by other clubs across the continent, and his style of play has been an important factor in making this decision.

"His achievements in Spain have certainly been very impressive, and we're confident that he is the right man to lead our next chapter."

12TH AUGUST 2023
THE FIRST POINT OF MANY (1 PT)

AFC Bournemouth 1-1 West Ham United

People often say that the most important step in a journey is the first one, and perhaps the same can be said of points.

A tricky opening schedule to the 2023/24 season began with the visit of West Ham United to Vitality Stadium.

The Hammers were fresh off the back of a triumph in the final of the UEFA Europa Conference League against Fiorentina, and equally as keen to get the campaign off to a winning start.

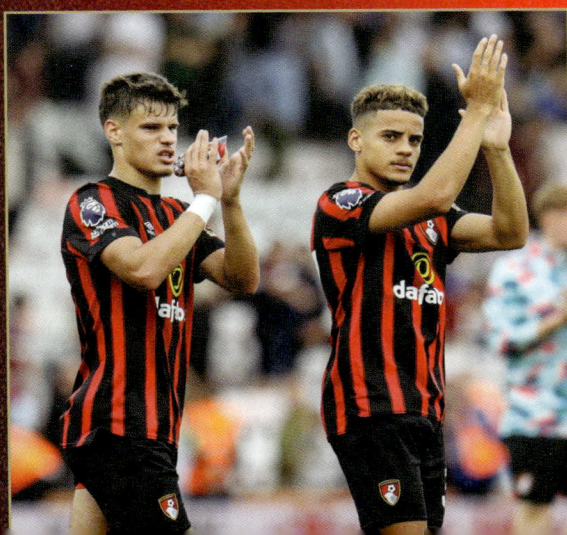

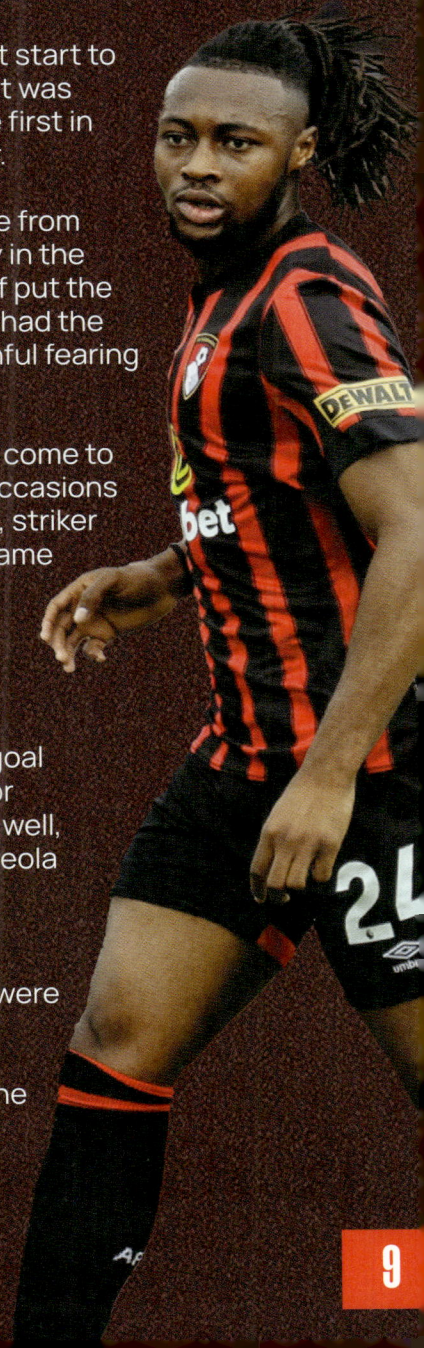

Meetings with Liverpool, Spurs, Brentford, Chelsea and Arsenal were to soon follow for the Cherries, so early points were of high importance to the team.

Despite a dominant start to the game though, it was West Ham to score first in the season opener.

A sensational strike from Jarrod Bowen early in the game's second half put the visitors ahead and had the Bournemouth faithful fearing the worst.

However, as would come to pass on so many occasions across the season, striker Dominic Solanke came to the rescue!

Piling on the pressure for an equaliser, Antoine Semenyo fired at goal from range, only for Solanke to control well, round Alphonse Areola and slot home the leveller.

Pre-match hopes were for three, but one point was better than zero to kick the season off!

A CRUCIAL VICTORY AGAINST THE CLARETS (6 PTS)

AFC Bournemouth 2-1 Burnley

For any football team, a first win is equally as important as that first point, and the Cherries certainly had to wait for it.

Feeling the effects of that tricky opening run of games to the season, it wasn't until the end of October that a first top-flight win arrived.

With both sides occupying spots in the relegation zone, Burnley travelled south with a victory of paramount importance to both teams.

Early in the game, it looked like it would be the Clarets that would nick it, too!

Just past the ten-minute mark, Charlie Taylor slammed in a superb half-volley from the edge of the Bournemouth box.

Knowing the importance of the game though, the Cherries showed huge spirit to fight back and quickly draw level.

Winning possession high up the pitch, Semenyo went on a powerful driving run that he would become known for as the season unfolded.

His run ended in a sliding left-footed finish and the scores were back level, but the home side needed more to get the points needed to spring the season into life.

In a hard-fought game, Iraola's side needed someone to step up and provide a special moment to win the game, and Philip Billing did just that!

Spotting James Trafford off his line a long, long way out from goal, the Danish midfielder let rip and beautifully found the back of the net from not far inside the Burnley half.

The stellar strike proved the difference on a rainy day in Dorset, and the club's first league win of the 23/24 season was sealed.

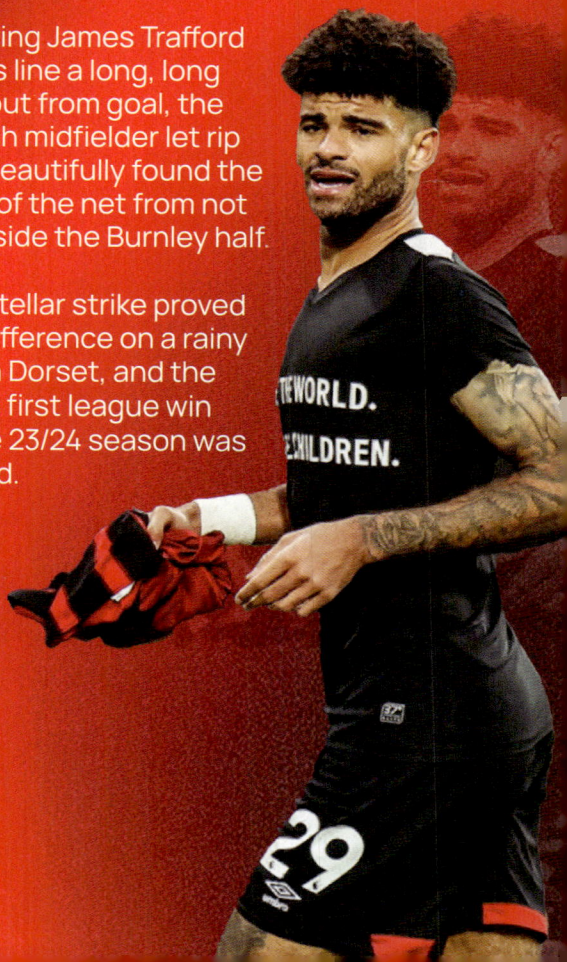

A dominant Bournemouth performance was to follow though, with the Sky cameras in attendance under the lights for an evening kick-off.

Semenyo, Justin Kluivert and Ryan Christie all forced good saves out of Nick Pope before the deadlock was finally broken.

The Cherries had to wait until the second half and Solanke was the man to do it, latching onto a loose ball before slamming home hard and low.

One very quickly became two, too, with the English striker acrobatically finishing at the near post following a corner.

11TH NOVEMBER 2023
A BIG WIN TO START A BIG RUN (9 PTS)

AFC Bournemouth 2-0 Newcastle United

Having had to wait for his first victory in the Premier League, the boss soon got to enjoy his second.

Despite defeats to Liverpool and Manchester City in the Carabao Cup and Premier League in between the visits of Burnley and Newcastle United to Vitality Stadium, the Cherries remained positive.

With the Toon battling it out in the Champions League and on the hunt for more European football in the 2024/25 term, Eddie Howe's side provided a difficult task.

The 2-0 triumph showed what the team was capable of and more important than the three points was the momentum it began for Iraola's team.

Victory over the Toon was the first game unbeaten in a streak of seven in the top-flight, six of which were wins, rocketing the club up the Premier League table.

9TH DECEMBER 2023
SILENCING 70,000 (19 PTS)

Manchester United 0-3 AFC Bournemouth

On that run of seven league matches unbeaten was one of the best results in the club's history!

Buoyed by a midweek win over Crystal Palace, the Cherries travelled to Old Trafford, having never won there.

The Red Devils certainly weren't at their best but on home turf posed a huge test for Iraola and his team.

In a typically wet and windy Manchester though, Bournemouth were fast out of the traps and silenced the United faithful inside five minutes.

Lewis Cook pressed high to win back possession before expertly picking out Solanke and he delicately flicked home.

The one-goal lead felt like dreamland for the Cherries, and it was protected at all costs with bodies on the line from the determined defence.

In the second half, things went from good to sensational as a quickfire double from Philip and Marcos Senesi put the away side out of sight of the Premier League giants.

But for a harshly disallowed Dango Ouattara goal in the final minutes, too, the result could have been even better!

The Cherries, who were well into their stride in the top flight now, settled for the three-goal margin, which made for one of the most memorable days in Bournemouth history.

What the gaffer said: "I feel very lucky to be here in front of these players!

"We are improving but we still have room to grow. We are solid defensively and we are now taking the rewards."

This second time around though, Iraola's side and tactics had gelled, and City's trip south offered a chance at unlikely revenge.

The class of the eventual title winners was clear, fresh off the back of their treble the previous season, as they put themselves a goal ahead in the opening half.

Neto denied an Erling Haaland strike only for Phil Foden to be in position to put the Manchester club ahead.

From there, the Cherries gave as good as they got and were a whisker away from an equaliser on several occasions.

A leveller was lacking despite the pressure though, and the game ended in defeat.

Although zero points were added to the tally, the performance against the world champions showed how far Iraola's team had progressed since the first half of the season and was perhaps a sign of things to come!

24TH FEBRUARY 2024
GIVING THE BEST IN THE WORLD A RUN FOR THEIR MONEY (28 PTS)

AFC Bournemouth 0-1 Manchester City

While the visit of Pep Guardiola's Manchester City didn't add to the season's points total, it did show the team's progression.

Earlier in the campaign, a trip to the Etihad ended in a 6-1 triumph for the hosts during the Cherries' difficult start to the season.

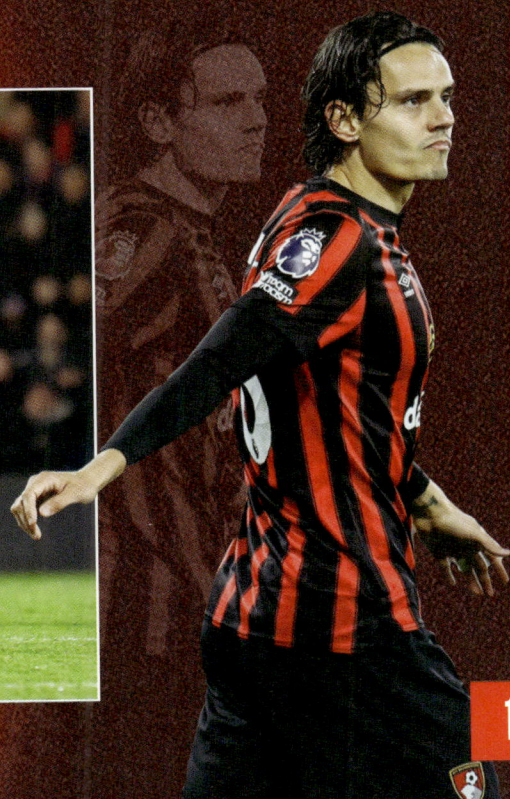

13TH MARCH 2024
BECOMING THE COMEBACK KINGS (35 PTS)

AFC Bournemouth 4-3 Luton Town

Not only were club records broken during the 2023/24 season, but Premier League records, too!

When Luton Town came to Bournemouth in mid-March following the suspension of the initial fixture, no one would have predicted what was to come.

A sluggish start saw the Hatters race into a deserved 3-0 lead come the break – stunning the Cherries on home turf.

After regrouping at half-time, the Cherries looked a different team in the second half and were level inside 20 minutes.

Solanke struck first after some clever skill before an Illia Zabarnyi header pulled another back.

Semenyo then took centre stage and two minutes on from Zabarnyi's goal, he drove inside from the right and slammed home a left-footed finish.

Three points were sealed in the game's final ten minutes as Semenyo struck again, the second time after being slipped in by Enes Ünal and the powerful finish gave Thomas Kaminski no chance.

The turnaround from three goals down at half-time was only the third time it had ever been done in Premier League history.

Claiming the awards:
The victory later won the league's Most Improbable Comeback award for 23/24 and contributed to Iraola claiming the Premier League Manager of the Month award for March!

28TH APRIL 2024
MISSION ACCOMPLISHED (48 PTS)

AFC Bournemouth 3-0 Brighton & Hove Albion

After the first step on the path to the points total was taken at home to West Ham in August, the final step was again on home soil, but with Brighton's visit in April.

A season's worth of work all came together against the Seagulls and Iraola's team blew Brighton away.

Roberto De Zerbi's side had enjoyed another impressive season, playing in Europe and aiming to qualify again, but were met by a determined Cherries performance.

Inside 15 minutes, Senesi flicked home at the near post following a corner and got the home side's momentum going.

A host of good chances came and went for Bournemouth before going two goals up in the second half, Ünal being the

man to net the second after meeting a pinpoint cross from Ouattara.

Justin Kluivert then completed the rout in the game's closing stages, powering infield from the right before hammering home with his left foot.

The three points took Iraola and the team beyond the tally of 46 earned in the 2016/17 Premier League season and secured their place in the history books.

While no further points were recorded in difficult fixtures against Arsenal, Brentford and Chelsea, the season as a whole is one that will live long in the memory!

Andoni's thoughts: "We played really well. It's difficult to play against Brighton, they have a lot of the ball, and you have to keep your composure and wait for your chances. It was a complete game.

"I'm very happy with the 48 points and we have to continue pushing."

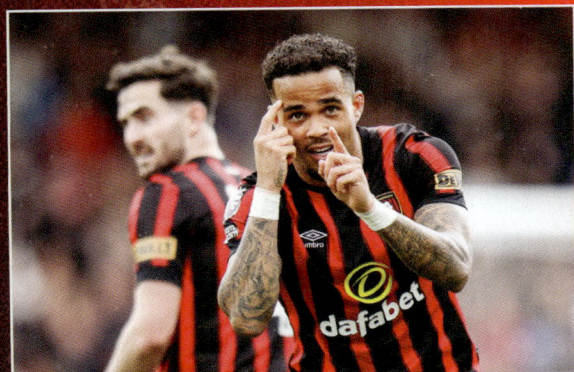

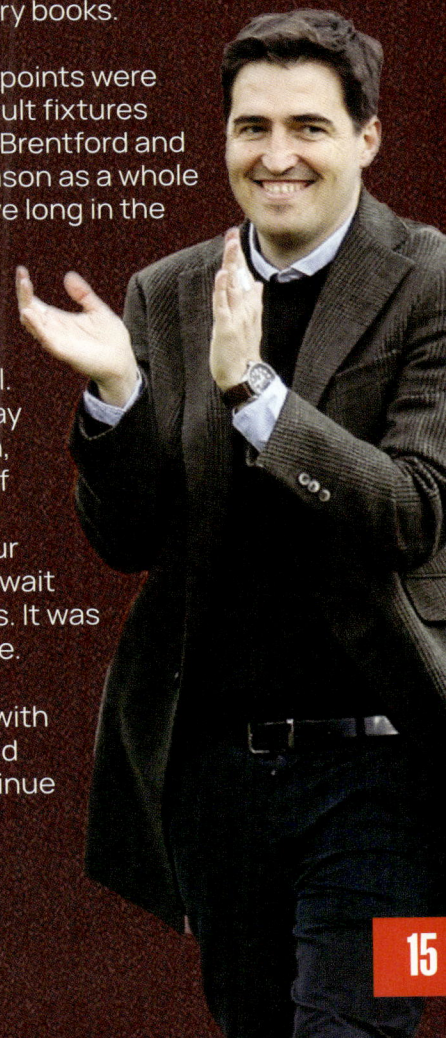

15

A DAY IN THE LIFE
MALACHI OGUNLEYE

With around eight billion people on the planet, one 24-hour period can be experienced in vastly different ways.

That can depend on the country you live in, the school you go to, your job or even vary between which team you play for at AFC Bournemouth.

So here, under-18 midfielder Malachi Ogunleye sheds a little light on what an average day in his life looks like...

7.15AM

First thing in the morning, I get washed and head downstairs for breakfast. I have oats with blueberries, bananas and nuts, that's my favourite breakfast meal.

Then, I head back upstairs, get changed into my training kit and pack my bag ready for the day.

Just before I leave, I say a prayer to God to ask to protect me and help me have a successful day.

8AM

I passed my driving test in January 2024, so I drive to training or get in with one of my teammates. I'm in digs with Ryan Carroll so we tend to share the driving.

8.30AM

The squad meets at The Hamworthy Club for breakfast. I have a small fruit bowl to top up what I had earlier.

9.15AM

We head to either Canford Park Arena or the new training ground. We have certain groups in the changing rooms, and we all have set jobs to do. It might be getting the gym ready or taking the medical kit out to the training ground.

10.15AM

We start our pre-activation which is mobility and stretching work to make sure we feel fresh for the session.

10.45AM-12.45PM

During training, we do lots of different drills. It starts with a warm-up where we may play some games like handball, tag or have races. That gets the vibe going.

We'll do a technical drill to flush out our legs then we will go into a possession-based drill with the focus on reactions. We also have a small-sided game depending on numbers. Towards the end, there are optional individual development programmes where you can practice what you think you need to practice.

After training, we go to the gym to do a lower or upper-body session.

1.45PM

It's back to The Hamworthy Club for lunch. My favourite option is pasta bake and most of the lads favour it. After lunch, we'll chill for a bit with our teammates and coaches and, sometimes, we will have a team meeting, normally when it's matchday minus one.

3.45PM

After that, I go back to my digs and have an online lesson. I join a call with three others who are studying A-level economics under the Premier League's education programme. It lasts about 90 minutes and I thoroughly enjoy it.

(As well as playing and training for the Cherries under-18s, Ogunleye is working towards a Level 3 BTEC Extended Diploma in Sport at Brockenhurst College and an A-level in economics.)

6PM

We all sit down for dinner, it's Ryan, me and Steve and Debbie from my digs. We always eat together and one of my favourite meals is curry and rice.

6.30PM

After dinner, I go on Huddle which is where we can watch back games and training. I like to review things so it's nice to be able to watch it back.

Also in the evenings, I like to catch up on some BTEC Extended Diploma stuff which I'm doing at Brockenhurst College.

I might work on an assignment or catch up on something else. Once the work is done, I'll go on my PlayStation and relax with my friends from back home in Southampton.

10PM

I always like to get a good night's sleep. I do my night-time routine, say a prayer and then go to bed.

COLOUR ME IN!

Have some fun with these Cherries-themed colouring pages and show off your skills! Give our badge and home kit a new look and see what you can come up with... make them any colours you want!

AFC BOURNEMOUTH

INTERNATIONAL CHERRIES

During the club's 125 years of history, players from all over the world have represented the Cherries.

With nearly 200 countries across seven continents on the planet, a football team can be made up of plenty of nationalities!

In last year's annual, we looked at the home nations of AFC Bournemouth players from across South America, Europe and Africa.

And here we trip across the world again to see where a different set of Cherries heroes from the men's and women's team come from outside of the UK.

TYLER ADAMS, USA

Midfielder Tyler Adams was born in Wappinger, New York, in the United States of America in 1999.

He began his career in his native country with New York Red Bulls before making a move to Europe for German outfit RB Leipzig.

After three and a half years in Leipzig, Adams made England his home by switching to Leeds United for a season before arriving in Bournemouth.

Adams has made over 40 appearances for his national side, gaining the captaincy in recent years alongside the nickname 'Captain America'!

THE USA

Capital city: Washington, D.C.
Population: 335 million
Official language: English
Currency: US Dollar
CONCACAF Gold Cups won: 7
Most capped player: Cobi Jones

FUN FACT

There are 50 stars on the USA's flag, which refer to the country's 50 states!

KENNI THOMPSON, BERMUDA

Cherries winger Kenni Thompson signed for the women's team in January of 2024.

She arrived in England from Spain, where the forward was playing for La Liga outfit SD Eibar.

Thompson also spent her younger years playing in the youth ranks of Spanish sides RCD Espanyol and FC Barcelona!

Making her debut in December 2023, Thompson represents the North Atlantic island of Bermuda on the international stage.

BERMUDA

Capital city: Hamilton
Population: 64,000
Official language: English
Currency: Bermuda Dollar
Women's Island Games gold medals: 1

FUN FACT

Bermuda has no rivers, lakes or freshwater springs so collecting rainwater is essential and is a requirement for every building on the island!

LUIS SINISTERRA, COLOMBIA

Luis Sinisterra was born in Santander de Quilichao, Colombia, in 1999 and started his career with Colombian side Once Caldas. Now playing on the south coast of England, the winger has also played his football in the Netherlands.

He left his home nation in 2018 for Europe, spending four years with Feyenoord before signing for Leeds United and then the Cherries. With over 15 international caps to his name, Sinisterra made his debut for Colombia in a 3-0 friendly defeat to Algeria in October 2019.

COLOMBIA

Capital city: Bogotá
Population: 52 million
Official language: Spanish
Currency: Colombian Peso
Copa Américas won: 1
Most capped player: David Ospina

FUN FACT

Colombia is the second most biodiverse country in the world, and one of just 17 'megadiverse' countries! 1/10th of all species on Earth can be found there due to its varied eco-systems.

EUROPE

GEMMA MCGUINNESS, IRELAND

Born in the coastal town of Moville, Ireland, Gemma McGuinness is one of the Cherries' European contingent. Moville is located in County Donegal in Ulster, which is one of four provinces in Ireland.

Before leaving her homeland to play in Bournemouth red and black, McGuinness represented Derry City, Sligo Rovers and Galway United. She's also played for the Girls in Green – Ireland's women's national team – at under-17 and under-19 level.

IRELAND

Capital city: Dublin
Population: 5 million
Official languages: English and Gaelic
Currency: Euro
Women's World Cups qualified for: 1
Most capped women's player: Emma Byrne

FUN FACT

It's estimated that over 10% of the Irish population have red hair, which is a higher percentage than any other country in the world!

JUSTIN KLUIVERT, THE NETHERLANDS

Cherries winger Justin Kluivert was born in the Dutch capital city of Amsterdam in May 1999. As the city hosting the biggest club in the Netherlands, the forward graduated through the academy ranks of that club, AFC Ajax.

From there, Kluivert embarked on an adventure across Europe, playing for clubs in Italy, Germany, France and Spain before arriving in England in the summer of 2023. When he scored his first Premier League goal for the Cherries, he became only the third player in history to score in Europe's top five leagues, and by far the youngest at that!

THE NETHERLANDS

Capital city: Amsterdam
Population: 18 million
Official language: Dutch
Currency: Euro
Euros won: 1
Most capped player: Wesley Sneijder

FUN FACT

As huge cyclists, the Dutch have more bicycles in the Netherlands than there are people! With a population in the region of 18 million, there are over 22 million bikes.

ENES ÜNAL, TURKEY

Turkish-born Enes Ünal is another Cherries hero who has called several countries across Europe home during his playing career.

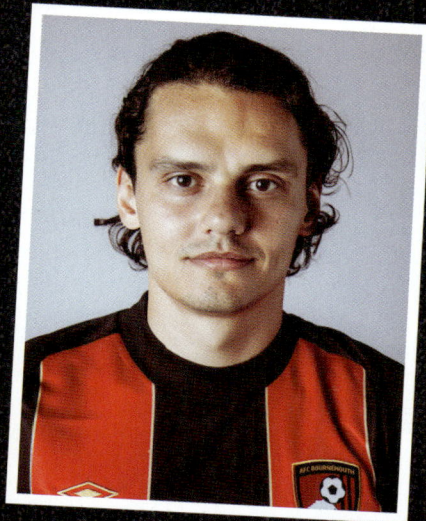

Starting out at his boyhood club Bursaspor in Turkey, he then made a big money move to Manchester City in 2015.

From there, Ünal had loans to clubs in Belgium and the Netherlands before relocating permanently to Spain for six and a half years ahead of signing for AFC Bournemouth. Having made his international debut as a 17-year-old, he has gone on to make over 30 appearances for Turkey.

TURKEY

Capital city: Ankara
Population: 86 million
Official language: Turkish
Currency: Turkish Lira
World Cups qualified for: 2
Most capped player: Rüştü Reçber

FUN FACT

Not to be confused with the football club, but Turkey is the largest producer of cherries in the world, with 500,000 tons of the fruit harvested there in a year!

QUESTION CORNER:
MARCUS TAVERNIER

As a Premier League footballer, there is a constant stream of questions to answer. Most of the time, those questions are about performance or whether the team has won or lost a match. Here, Cherries winger Marcus Tavernier answers some questions with a difference, having been sent in by Bournemouth fans!

Do you have a set routine or superstitions you like to do before walking down the tunnel, coming out onto the pitch?

I normally have a drink with me when I go out onto the pitch, it's always a full drink and I have it with me for the game.

Last season, I started standing in front of Dom Solanke – about half-way through the season I did that.

I'm not really sure why, to be honest! I was probably hoping he'd rub some of his luck onto me to score more goals, which didn't work too much!

My third one is I always tie my shorts in the tunnel and then I hop over the line when I enter the pitch, I've always done that.

How was it adapting to Andoni's style of football and how has it helped you improve as a footballer?

It's been great, not only for me but for the whole team.

It was a learning curve at the start and every player in the team would say that we found it tough. We weren't getting the key details right and it wasn't anyone's fault, these things take time to learn and become fluid.

The manager was great, he explained it and kept trying to help us change and perform better on the pitch and it clicked for us all and we had a good season last season.

He's really helped change us to create chances and score goals and it's tough to play in but it's great.

Why do I always meg him in training? (Alex Scott)

What, that question is from Scotty? Seriously? Alex Scott!? He has NEVER megged me in training, he needs to wake up!

What is your favourite motorway service station?

That's interesting! Weatherby up north, I think.

They have a famous fish and chip shop called the Weatherby Whaler a little further out, so I'm going to say there. Interesting question, though!

How are them turkey sandwiches?

I didn't have too many last season, they're the best sandwiches though and I probably need to start bringing them back!

Would you rather be made of biscuit or cake? And which specific biscuit or cake?

Hmmm... Probably biscuit. Bit stronger, I guess. I'd go for Biscoff as well as I've always liked that one.

If you had to choose... baseball with your brother James Tavernier or a round of golf with Rory McIlroy?

That's an easy one that, baseball with my brother would be great fun. Got to keep it in the family as well!

Do you play Warzone?

Warzone is exactly what I play. I'd like to think when I retire, I might become a professional... I'm not that good yet though! I'm fully focussed on the football as well!

Who's got the best music taste in the squad?

Apart from myself, Antoine Semenyo has the same style as me. It's always good music and it's good for gym sessions and just general good vibes!

Ideal five-a-side team, past or present?

Tough one that, I might just go for a team fully from the past, but there's some legends still playing! Not sure how to tackle this one...

Sweeper keeper? I don't want a permanent goalkeeper, I'll go with one defender I think, let's go very attacking.

My defender is Sergio Ramos. How hard is this to pick five!?

Ronaldo and Messi are my two strikers, that's simple. Both unbelievable.

I'm actually going to put myself in there, I want to play with these players! Imagine.

Then I think I'll round it off with Yaya Toure. What a player he was when he finished off in the Premier League. That's a strong team that!

Although I didn't pick my brother... maybe he can manage the team!

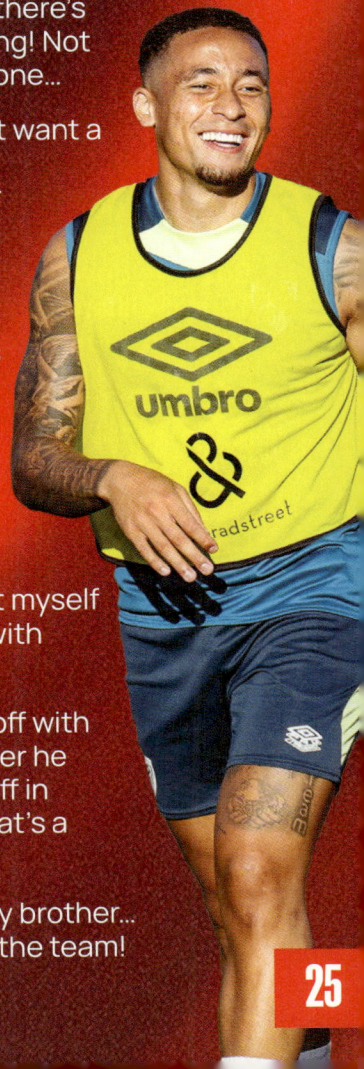

A DAY IN THE LIFE

TOURE WILLIAMS

With around eight billion people on the planet, one 24-hour period can be experienced in vastly different ways.

That can depend on the country you live in, the school you go to, your job or even vary between which team you play for at AFC Bournemouth.

So here, development squad midfielder Toure Williams sheds a little light on what an average day in his life looks like...

7.45AM

I stay in digs in Bournemouth during the season.

In the mornings, I like to keep it simple. I wake up, wash my face and brush my teeth before I leave to go to training.

8.30AM

I will normally get to the stadium at this time for breakfast. I will either have scrambled eggs or poached eggs on toast depending on how I feel, with a glass of orange juice.

To get myself ready for the day I will normally have eggs, but my favourite breakfast would be pancakes. If it was a special occasion, I would be having pancakes with lots of sauce!

9.45AM

We will get to Canford to get ready for training, do some prehab and some stretching. I will meet up with the boys and talk about what's going to happen that day.

3.30PM

I will probably go home and relax a little bit. My digs has a dog, so I will sit with him for a little bit and watch some TV.

5.30PM

I will make myself some dinner, my go-to dinner would probably be barbeque chicken thighs and rice.

6.30PM

I will shower after dinner, and this is where I have probably done everything I need to do for the day. From then I am just unwinding. I will probably go on my laptop and play Football Manager.

10.00PM

Normally, I'll go to bed at this time and aim to be asleep by 10.30pm. I usually go to sleep quite quickly.

After a hard day, getting as much sleep as you can is important, so you are ready to go again for another day.

10.30AM

Training will normally start at this time with different drills for us to do. That's where we work with the coaches to try to improve every day.

Depending on the day, training would be either match preparation or, if it's midweek, a harder session. It will always be related to yourself and how we are going to play as a team.

1PM

Normally, at this time, training will be done, and we will head back to the stadium for lunch.

We will all have lunch at the stadium as a group, that's always really nice.

2.30PM

We will then head to the gym or do a bit of analysis. That could be watching training clips and looking at what we did well, or seeing how we could improve. It could also be how things we have done in training are related to the games.

125 FOR 125

The 2024/25 season comes as an extra special one for AFC Bournemouth and all associated with the club! Founded in 1899, the season sees the Cherries celebrate a huge 125 years of existence. With a massive amount of history and statistics packed into all those years, here are 125 totally random facts about the club...

1 AFC Bournemouth's first promotion came during the 1970/71 season, from Division Four to Division Three.

2 The club has gained eight promotions throughout its entire history.

3 The club first started playing at its Dean Court home in 1910.

4 The Cherries hit the headlines during the 1982/83 season when they signed legendary attacking midfielder George Best. He played five times in the league for the club after joining from San Jose Earthquakes.

5 Ted MacDougall first arrived at AFC Bournemouth from York City for a reported £10,000 in the summer of 1969.

6 Callum Wilson became the first player to score a top-flight hat-trick for the Cherries, when he netted a treble against West Ham United in August 2015.

7 Andoni Iraola managed the Cherries to their greatest ever Premier League points tally during the 2023/24 season, with 48 in total.

8 AFC Bournemouth registered 26 wins in the league during their famous Championship-winning campaign in 2014/15.

9 The club overcame Birmingham City 8-0 during that successful, title-winning season. The club's biggest-ever league victory.

10 Frizzell insurance first became the club's official shirt sponsor during the 1993/94 season.

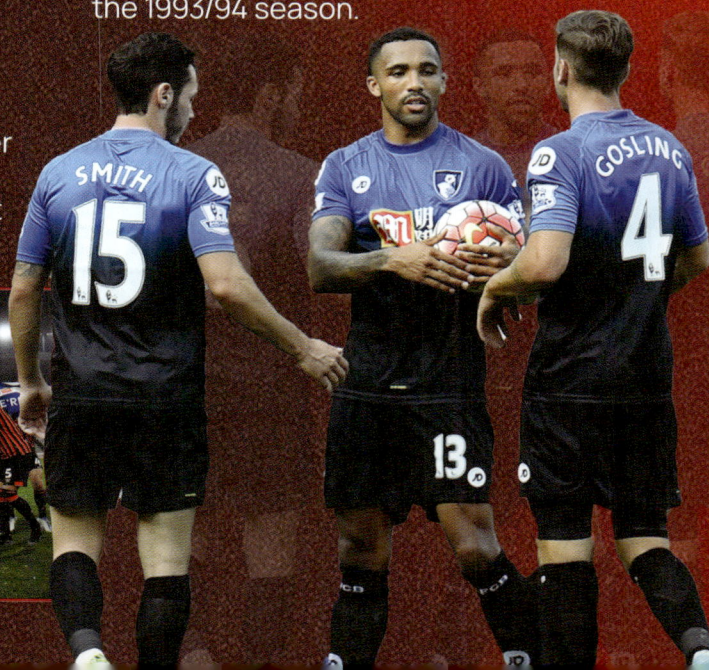

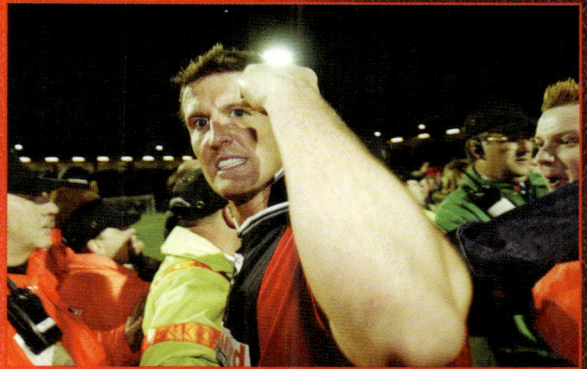

11 Chris Mepham played his first international game as a Cherries player, when Wales took on Slovakia in March 2019.

12 AFC Bournemouth beat Port Vale 4-0 in the final home game of their 2009/10 League Two promotion-winning campaign.

13 Artur Boruc made his debut for the Cherries against Watford in September 2014, having initially joined the club on loan from Southampton.

14 Matt Ritchie's sparkling form for AFC Bournemouth earned him a call-up to the Scotland squad. He made his international debut against Northern Ireland in a friendly in March 2015.

15 Reg Haynes Toyota were the club's official shirt sponsors during the 1981/82 promotion-winning season.

16 John Bond succeeded Freddie Cox as the club's manager in May 1970.

17 The club has been known by three different names since its formation in 1899. Boscombe FC became Bournemouth & Boscombe Athletic Football Club upon entry to the Football League in 1923, and since 1972 has been known as AFC Bournemouth.

18 Dan Gosling was the first player to score a Boxing Day goal for the Cherries in the Premier League. His strike came against West Ham in a 3-3 draw in 2017.

19 Darren Anderton scored 13 goals during his time as a Cherries player, having first signed for the club in September 2006.

20 Sir Matt Busby, the legendary Manchester United manager, was a guest player for the Cherries during 1945/46.

21 Striker Steve Fletcher holds the club's appearance record, having played 628 times in two spells between July 1992 and July 2007, and January 2009 and May 2013.

22 The club's first professional player was Boscombe-born Baven Penton in 1912 and his weekly wage was 30 shillings (£1.50).

23 The Cherries triumphed 5-2 against Lincoln City to win the Division Three play-off final at the Millennium Stadium in Cardiff in May 2003.

24 Cherries defender Baily Cargill marked his debut for England under-20s by scoring in a 2-2 draw against Canada at Vitality Stadium in November 2014.

25 Matt Holland once played for the Cherries with a broken arm, a post-match x-ray revealing the midfielder had sustained the fracture.

26 Nathan Aké was the club's only ever-present Premier League starter during the 2018/19 campaign.

27 The Cherries hold the record for the longest continuous stay in the third tier of English football. After playing their first-ever league game in the Third Division (South) at the start of the 1923/24 season, the club remained in Division 3 until 1970, when it suffered relegation to the Fourth Division.

28 A 3-3 draw at Luton in December 2008 saw the Cherries finally wipe out their 17-point deduction and move on to zero points during the Great Escape season.

29 Charlie Daniels' stunning volley against Manchester City won him the Premier League goal-of-the-month award in August 2017.

30 A star-studded Real Madrid team, including Cristiano Ronaldo, Luka Modrić and Mesut Özil and managed by Carlo Ancelotti, cruised to a 6-0 win against the Cherries in a friendly at Vitality Stadium in 2013.

31 Harry Arter joined AFC Bournemouth from Woking for just £4,000 in 2010. He made his 256th and final appearance for the club in a Carabao Cup clash against Crystal Palace in September 2020.

32 The first Football League game at Dean Court took place on 1st September 1923 and was against Swindon Town. The match ended goalless in front of a crowd of around 7,000.

33 Goals from Nathan Aké, Harry Wilson and Callum Wilson saw the Cherries win 3-1 against Southampton at St Mary's – the Cherries' first victory over their rivals in the city in September 2019.

34 Former Cherries youngster Sam Vokes netted a memorable goal for Wales against Belgium in Euro 2016 to take them to their first ever semi-final of a major tournament.

35 Reg Cutler almost caused the abandonment of the Cherries' 1956/57 FA Cup fourth round tie against Wolves when he crashed into the goalpost which led to the goal collapsing. After it had been repaired, Cutler scored the only goal to earn the Cherries one of their most famous cup wins.

36 The club's first major trophy success came in May 1946, when the Cherries defeated Walsall 1-0 in the Third Division (South) Cup final at Stamford Bridge.

37 Now having managed in both England and Scotland, Stephen Robinson joined the Cherries from Tottenham Hotspur in October 1994 and scored 51 league goals for the club before signing for Preston North End in May 2000.

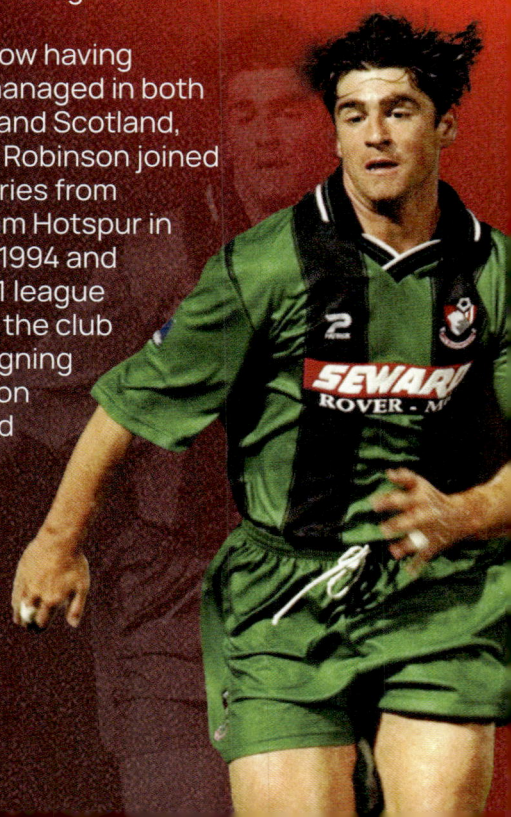

38 Defender Shaun Teale made 100 league appearances for the Cherries between January 1989 and July 1991 and was named player of the year in 1989/90 and 1990/91.

39 Jimmy White is the club's youngest debutant, having featured in a 3-1 win over Port Vale in April 1958 aged 15 years and 321 days.

40 The Cherries heaviest defeat in the FA Cup is 7-0 – against Sheffield Wednesday in January 1932 and Burnley in January 1965.

41 Initially signed on loan from Grays Athletic, Mark Molesley's move to the Cherries was made permanent when the midfielder became Eddie Howe's first signing in management in January 2009.

42 Former England defender Rio Ferdinand joined the Cherries on loan from West Ham during the 1996/97 season, making ten appearances in total.

43 The Cherries first signed Tony Pulis from Newport County in 1986 before he later went on to manage the club.

44 The first and only player measuring 6ft 9in to be registered with the Football League was Boscombe's reserve goalkeeper Bill Carr, in 1924/25.

45 Boscombe played three Third Division (South) games at the start of the ill-fated 1939/40 season. In one of these, they beat Northampton Town at Dean Court 10-0, but all the results were expunged from the records.

46 Harry Redknapp spotted Efan Ekoku and brought him to the club from Sutton United in the summer of 1990.

47 Wade Elliott joined the Cherries from non-league Bashley in February 2000 and helped the club win promotion at the Millennium Stadium in 2003. He then signed for Burnley in July 2005.

48 Glenn Murray's late goal earned the Cherries a famous 1-0 victory against reigning Premier League champions Chelsea at Stamford Bridge in December 2015.

49 James Hayter wrote his own chapter in footballing folklore by scoring the fastest hat-trick in the history of the EFL, as the Cherries put six unanswered goals past Wrexham in February 2004.

50 The Cherries' biggest win in competitive football was against Southern League Margate in the first round of the FA Cup in November 1971. Ted MacDougall scored nine of the goals and the other two came from Mel Machin and Micky Cave.

51 Manchester United old boy Joshua King scored the only goal against his former club as the Cherries beat the former Premier League champions in November 2019.

52 Nathan Aké joined AFC Bournemouth for a reported club-record fee of £20m from Chelsea in the summer of 2017.

53 Bournemouth failed to score in 20 of their 46 league games in the 1995/96 season. They finished 14th in the third tier.

54 Luther Blissett scored an impressive 19 league goals during his first season with AFC Bournemouth, having signed for the club in 1988.

55 Aaron Ramsdale's impressive pre-season form earned the goalkeeper his Premier League debut for the Cherries against former club Sheffield United in August 2019.

56 The club signed Lewis Cook from Leeds United on a four-year deal for a reported fee of £7m in July 2016. He would go on to lift the Under-20 World Cup as captain of England the following summer.

57 The Cherries' longest-ever cup tie took place during the 1974/75 season. Their League Cup second round tie against Hartlepool United consisted of four games. After the first three had been drawn, visitors Bournemouth won the fourth 1-0.

58 As Boscombe FC, the club first competed in the FA Cup during the 1909/10 season.

59 Ian Cox made 172 league appearances for the Cherries after signing from Crystal Palace in March 1996 before leaving for Burnley in February 2000.

60 Earlier in his career, Italy's Roberto Mancini and Argentina's Lionel Scaloni were impressed by Marcos Senesi. With him eligible to play for either nation, he received a call-up from both. The Cherries defender opted to represent Argentina.

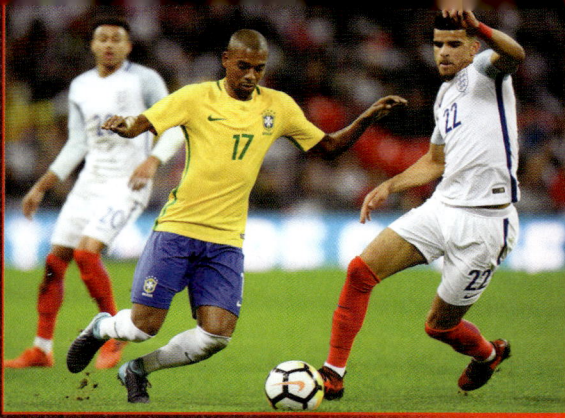

61 Brian Stock scored the first goal in a 3-0 win over Wrexham in the first game played at the developed Dean Court in November 2001, after the pitch had been turned 90 degrees.

62 Long-serving right-back Neil Young made 429 league appearances for the Cherries between October 1994 and May 2008.

63 England international Danny Ings came through the youth ranks at the Cherries and was given his professional debut by Eddie Howe in October 2009.

64 Dominic Solanke was already an England senior international when he arrived at AFC Bournemouth in January 2019. He had featured in a friendly for the Three Lions against Brazil in November 2017.

65 During the Cherries famous FA Cup run in 1956/57, they were drawn against the First Division leaders in three successive rounds. Wolves and Spurs were beaten before Freddie Cox's side succumbed to Manchester United in the quarterfinals.

66 Midfielder Nigel Spackman started his career at non-league Andover before signing for the Cherries in 1980. He would go on to play for the likes of Chelsea, Liverpool and Rangers.

67 Dan Gosling featured 14 times in the league for Blackpool while on loan from Newcastle, before arriving at AFC Bournemouth in the summer of 2014.

68 David Brooks capped off a fine first season with the Cherries by scoring his inaugural international goals for Wales against Croatia in June 2019.

69 Born in Cape Town, striker Mark Stein joined the Cherries from Chelsea following a successful loan spell. His permanent signing came ahead of the 1998/99 season.

70 After signing from Hereford United in 2010, winger Marc Pugh's compensation fee went to a tribunal. The Cherries ended up paying £100,000, and Pugh would go on to become a legend at the club.

71 The first floodlit game to take place at Dean Court was a Third Division fixture against Northampton Town on 27th September 1961.

72 Midfielder Matt Holland started his youth career in the academies of Arsenal and West Ham United before joining the Cherries. He would go on to captain the side as well as playing 116 times.

73 AFC Bournemouth last played a fixture on both Christmas Day and Boxing Day during the 1957/58 campaign.

74 During the 2023/24 season, Jonny Stuttle scored a memorable hat-trick for the club's under-18s in the FA Youth Cup, as they sealed a 5-0 victory over Newcastle at St James' Park.

75 After losing their opening fixture, AFC Bournemouth then went on a run of seven consecutive league wins during the early stages of their 1970/71 promotion campaign.

76 Harry Cornick made his one and only Cherries senior appearance in a 5-1 victory over Rotherham United in the FA Cup in 2015.

77 England star Jack Wilshere played 27 times for Cherries in the Premier League during the 2016/17 campaign, having joined on a season-long loan. He helped Eddie Howe's men record their highest-ever league finish, ending the season ninth in the topflight.

78 Simon Francis was voted AFC Bournemouth's Supporters' Player of the Year following the club's first top-flight season in 2015/16.

79 The biggest crowd for a competitive game at Dean Court was 28,799 for the FA Cup quarter-final against Manchester United in March 1957.

80 Brett Pitman scored in eight consecutive league games for the Cherries between 12th March and 20th April 2012.

81 In season 1928/29, former Cherries manager Harry Kinghorn, who at the time was 42 years of age and the club's trainer, came out of retirement to play on the left wing in a league game against Brentford.

82 Mark Travers became the youngest goalkeeper to start a Premier League game since Joe Hart for Man City in 2006, when he made his Cherries debut against Tottenham in May 2019.

83 While the Cherries have been regular visitors to Manchester City's Etihad Stadium in recent years, they last visited City's former ground Maine Road during the 1998/99 season.

84 Warren Feeney was a full international with Northern Ireland during his time with the Cherries in the early 2000s.

85 Charlie Daniels came through the youth ranks at Tottenham Hotspur before eventually reaching the topflight as an AFC Bournemouth player.

86 Two Cherries players were named in the EFL Championship Team of the Season for 2014/15, Simon Francis and Matt Ritchie.

87 Charlton Athletic provided the opposition for Neil Young's testimonial in 2005.

88 Yann Kermorgant bagged a hat-trick on his full debut for the Cherries in a 5-0 win against Doncaster in March 2014 and played a starring role as the club lifted the Championship title in 2014/15.

89 AFC Bournemouth totalled 97 points in their 1986/87 Third Division title-winning season, the points haul saw them finish three ahead of runners-up Middlesbrough.

90 While playing for Stoke City in 2013, former Cherries goalkeeper Asmir Begović scored against another ex-AFC Bournemouth keeper Artur Boruc, who was in goal for Southampton at the time.

91 Lee Bradbury ended his lengthy playing career with the Cherries, having made 146 appearances for the club in total.

92 AC Milan provided star-studded opposition for Cherries ace Warren Cummings in his testimonial at Vitality Stadium in 2016.

93 The Cherries remained unbeaten at home during the 1962/63 season winning 11 and drawing 12 of their league games played at Dean Court.

94 Battling midfielder Jefferson Lerma was shown a total of 12 yellow cards for the club during the 2018/19 campaign.

95 Having joined the Cherries in 1993, striker Steve Cotterill netted 15 goals in his first season at Dean Court.

96 Preston North End were the opponents when Shaun Cooper played his final game for AFC Bournemouth in 2012.

97 Sir Alex Ferguson handed Russell Beardsmore his professional debut at Manchester United before he signed for AFC Bournemouth in 1993.

98 Maisy Smith lifted the Women's Hampshire Senior Cup following the Cherries' penalty shootout victory over Southampton RTC Academy at Fratton Park in May 2023, the first time the club had won the prestigious competition.

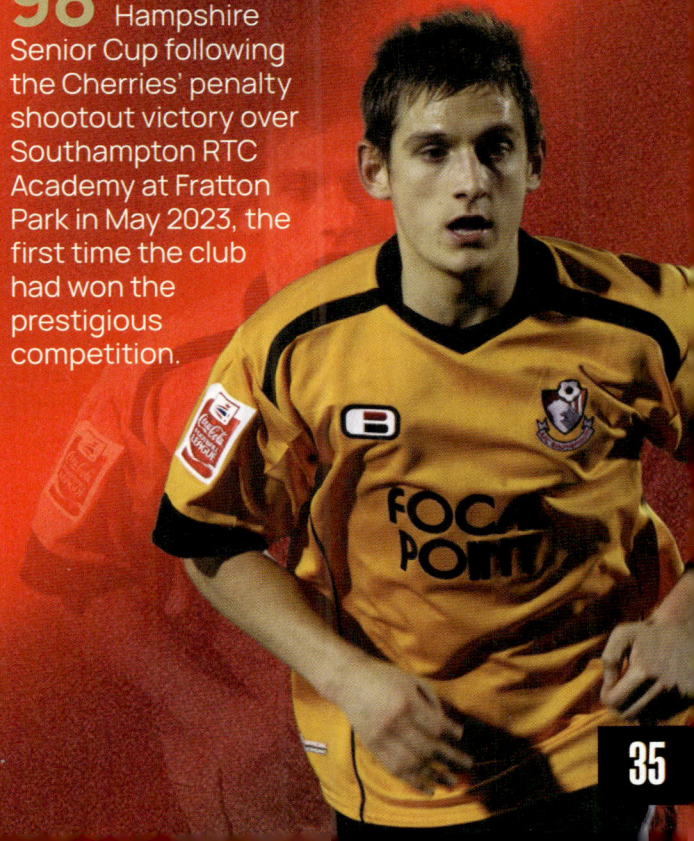

99 Jack Russell is the only player to score four goals in a league game for the Cherries on more than one occasion, against Clapton Orient in January 1933 and Bristol City three weeks later.

100 During the club's Great Escape season in 1994/95, the Cherries won six of their final nine league games to beat the drop in the Second Division.

101 Former Bristol City man Antoine Semenyo also spent time on loan at Bath City, Newport County and Sunderland in his earlier years before joining the Cherries in 2023.

102 Steve Fletcher played for Chesterfield and Crawley Town before his second spell under Eddie Howe at the Cherries in January 2009.

103 AFC Bournemouth's Kenni Thompson became the first women's player to win an international cap while on the club's books after she represented Bermuda.

104 AFC Bournemouth Women team won 19 of their 22 league games during the 2023/24 campaign but missed out on promotion in a final-day decider against rivals Exeter City.

105 Bournemouth & Boscombe's last competitive game on a Christmas Day was played in 1957 when they beat Reading 4-1 at Dean Court in front of 11,162 spectators.

106 The Cherries development squad recorded a third-place finish in their inaugural Professional Development League campaign in 2023/24, their first as a category two level academy.

107 Earlier in his career, AFC Bournemouth goalkeeper Neto was capped six times by Brazil at under-23 level and helped them win a silver medal at the 2012 Olympics in England

108 The 2023/24 season saw club legend Adam Smith surpass 350 appearances for AFC Bournemouth.

109 Alongside his famous father, Patrick, Cherries forward Justin Kluivert's grandfather Kenneth represented Suriname at international level, younger brother Ruben turned out for FC Utrecht and half-brother Shane has played in Barcelona's academy.

110 Ryan Christie made 151 appearances for Scottish giants Celtic, scoring 41 goals and setting up 44, before linking up with the Cherries on a permanent deal in August 2021.

111 Prior to joining the Cherries in the summer of 2022, Helen Bleazard had featured in the FA Women's Super League and played in two FA Women's Cup finals.

112 When the Cherries joined the Football League in 1923, the maximum wage for a senior professional footballer was £8 a week.

113 Holly Humphreys made her AFC Bournemouth Women debut when she started just four days after her 16th birthday in a 0-0 draw against Oxford United in the National League Cup in September 2022.

114 AFC Bournemouth development squad goalkeeper Mack Allan is the grandson of 1966 World Cup winner Alan Ball.

115 Bill Coxon became the first substitute used by the club when they were first allowed during the 1965/66 season.

116 Combative middleman Karlos Gregory, who represents the club's development squad, is a black belt in Taekwondo alongside his exploits in football.

117 Women's playmaker Molly Barron-Clark was voted as the best beach soccer player in the world in November 2021.

118 Andoni Iraola is the first head coach to manage the club from outside of the United Kingdom.

119 Under-18s midfielder Malachi Ogunleye was once a champion break dancer.

120 Callum Wilson netted a 90th-minute goal to secure the Cherries victory at Burnley on the final day of the 2017/18 season.

121 Striker Daniel Jebbison has represented England at three different youth levels. He was part of the 2022 UEFA European Under-19 Championship-winning squad.

122 Development squad midfielder Lewis Brown has a cousin called Fletcher Brown, who is named after Cherries legend Steve.

123 Cherries' resolute defence conceded only 30 goals in 46 league games during the 1981/82 season, when they gained promotion back up to the Third Division.

124 Signed from Chelsea in July 2006, midfielder Danny Hollands was voted the Cherries' player of the year in 2008 and joined Charlton Athletic in May 2011.

125 Jermain Defoe scored 18 league goals while on loan from West Ham during the 2000/01 season.

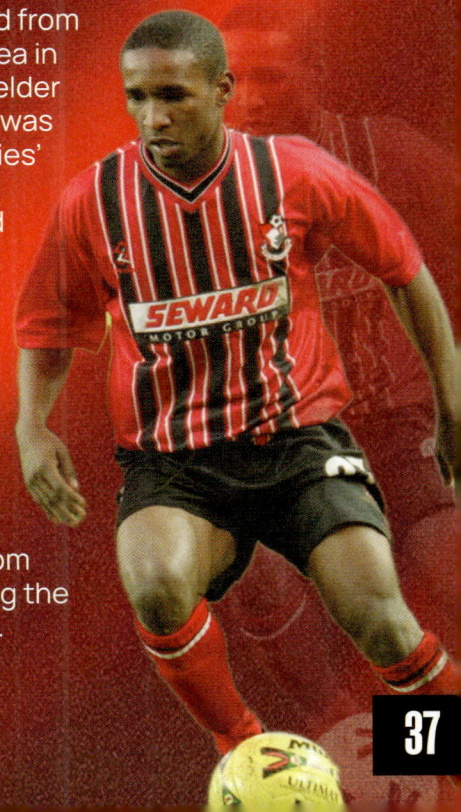

BOURNE IN THE USA

Ahead of the 2024/25 Premier League campaign, the Cherries headed to the United States of America for a pre-season tour. Based in the West Coast state of California, Andoni Iraola and his squad spent two weeks across the Atlantic Ocean. Here are some of what the squad got up to out in America alongside a chocka pre-season training schedule...

CLASSY KITS

A glitz and glamour tour needs a look to match, and part-owner Michael B. Jordan certainly provided the Hollywood feel...

The American actor and producer designed bespoke kits which the Cherries played in out in the States.

Two MBJ x AFCB strips – one in red and one in black – were launched and then worn for the games there.

MATCH ACTION

The first of the friendlies in the USA saw Iraola's team take on Ryan Reynolds and Rob McElhenney-owned Wrexham AFC in Santa Barbara. A Marcos Senesi goal for the Cherries in the second half saw the sides draw 1-1 at Harder Stadium.

Next up, there was an all-Premier League clash in Los Angeles, where the team was based for training at Dignity Health Sports Park, as we went head-to-head with Arsenal.

That game also finished in a 1-1 draw, with Fábio Vieira and Antoine Semenyo on the scoresheet before the Gunners finished on top in a penalty shootout.

Before the tour was over, a behind-closed-doors meeting with LA Galaxy was also played.

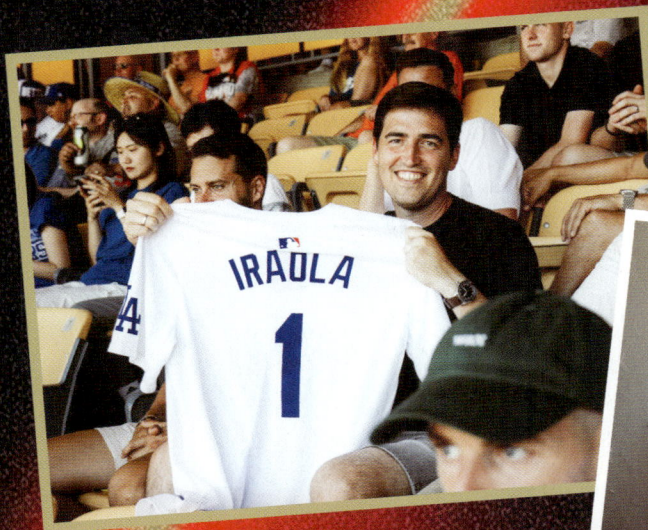

BOURNEMOUTH DOES BASEBALL

Another iconic American trip out saw the whole squad visit the home of baseball in Los Angeles.

The 56,000-seater Dodger Stadium hosted the lads for some Major League Baseball action.

On the day the Cherries were in attendance, the Dodgers were beaten 8-3 by the San Francisco Giants.

HAMED AND JUSTIN IN HOLLYWOOD

Making the most of the Californian surroundings, Cherries attackers Hamed Traorė and Justin Kluivert were taken on a tour of Hollywood.

The first stop was the iconic hillside sign, where the duo posed for a shoot and even bumped into football fans wanting pictures!

From there, they headed down to Sunset Boulevard and took a walk with the stars to find the one belonging to Michael B. Jordan.

CHERRIES STARS AT SHOE PALACE

Before flying back across the Atlantic Ocean, some of the lads had one last stop off in LA.

Shoe Palace is an iconic shopping destination in the States, and they held a Cherries takeover for the day.

Tyler Adams and Enes Ünal went down for a signing session to meet supporters, with Michael B. Jordan also making an appearance!

COLOUR ME IN!

Have some fun with these Cherries-themed colouring pages and show off your skills! Some of our boys have lost all their colours, see if you can bring them back!

A DAY IN THE LIFE

HELEN BLEAZARD

With around eight billion people on the planet, one 24-hour period can be experienced in vastly different ways.

That can depend on the country you live in, the school you go to, your job or even vary between which team you play for at AFC Bournemouth.

So here, women's first-team player Helen Bleazard sheds a little light on what an average day in her life looks like...

7.30AM

I wake up around 7.30am and have my Collagen thanks to Gemma McGuinness' nutritional advice! It's meant to be good for recovery.

I then have cereal for my breakfast or something else quite simple if I fancy a change.

8.30AM

I have to start work at 8.30am – I work for the housing association. I'm a Senior Neighbourhood Officer.

I have a little patch of houses to look after, and I look after some tenants.

In the morning, I would tend to go out and visit tenants in the local area and check in on any issues.

When I go out, I make sure I pack lots of water for hydration. I try to only be out for half a day, so I'm normally back for lunchtime.

6.30PM

In the evenings, it's then off to training for around 6.30pm down at Ringwood.

Sometimes that will consist of recovery or we'll focus more on the weekend's game depending on where we're at in the season.

If it's a training night, I'll have a snack before and then eat properly after. I like a lot of carbs to keep my energy up, so I'll have something like that with some meat.

12PM

Lunch would be scrambled eggs on toast, it's my favourite at the moment!

Once again, shoutout to Gemma McGuinness who says I need more protein in my diet. I wasn't eating enough before, so I also tend to have a protein yoghurt with it too.

My lunchtime varies... if it's a training day then I won't go to the gym, but if it isn't I tend to take myself down to The Village for a workout on my break.

It's a long season, so it's important to stay on top of my wellbeing and fitness, especially after I had an operation in the summer.

9PM

I'll then ice my ankle in the evening and do my stretches that the doc gave me to keep it strong.

I want to avoid re-injuring, so it's important I look after myself during this time.

9.30PM

Before bed, in the summer it's Love Island but I also love a detective programme!

There's always one recorded, so I'm never short of options.

1PM

The rest of my day will be admin or appointments, so the afternoon goes by really quickly.

IRAOLA IN NUMBERS

Cherries head coach Andoni Iraola arrived at Vitality Stadium in the summer of 2023 after leaving Rayo Vallecano. In his first season in charge, the AFC Bournemouth boss led the club to its record points total in the Premier League. Not only did the points tally win plaudits from fans and pundits alike, but his exciting and front-foot playing style did too! To get to know the head coach a bit more, here are some key stats from his life...

1982

The year the boss was born on **22nd June** in Usurbil, Spain.

13

In his first season as Cherries boss, he won **13** Premier League matches – our joint-most ever in one season.

1

The head coach has won **one** piece of silverware in his career as a manager, winning the Cypriot Super Cup in 2018.

48

Iraola led us to our record Premier League points tally in 2023/24, getting **48 points** in the top-flight!

18

While in Spain as a player, Iraola played against the legendary Lionel Messi **18** times, unfortunately for the boss, he didn't win any!

510

Primarily a right-back throughout his career, he was a tough tackler and an excellent passer, spending the majority of his playing days with Athletic Bilbao. He appeared in **510** matches in 12 seasons with his boyhood club.

3

He played as a youth for Antiguoko, alongside teammates such as Mikel Arteta, Xabi Alonso, Mikel Alonso and Aritz Aduriz. Including him, **three** have gone on to manage in the game professionally.

38

5

The memorable comeback against Luton last season, which Iraola was at the heart of, meant that we were only the **fifth** team in Premier league history to win after overcoming a three-goal deficit.

He played **38** times for New York City FC, managed by Arsenal icon Patrick Vieira as well as playing with legends of the game like David Villa, Frank Lampard and Andrea Pirlo.

7

An international footballer, the head coach played **seven** times for Spain between 2008 and 2011.

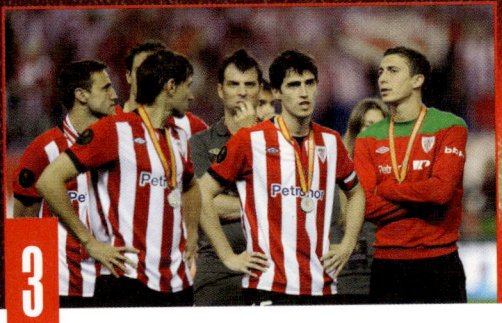

2

3

During his time with Mirandés in the Segunda Division in 2019, he reached the Spanish Cup semi-final for just the **second** time in their 92-year history, beating top-tier sides like Celta Vigo, Sevilla and Villarreal in an unbelievable cup run.

The boss was so close to winning **three** different trophies in his playing career, finishing as a runner-up five times. Three occasions were in the Copa del Rey (2008/09, 2011/12 and 2014/15), once in the Supercopa de España (2009) and once in the UEFA Europa League (2011/12).

TEN YEARS ON WITH
TOMMY

Tommy Elphick will go down in history as the first player to captain AFC Bournemouth to the Premier League.

The influential defender led from the front and played every game when the Cherries achieved the feat in 2014/15.

He lifted the trophy following a dramatic conclusion on the final day and capped a memorable season by being crowned Supporters' Player of the Year.

Although a 3-0 win over Bolton in their penultimate game had all but guaranteed promotion, the title was still up for grabs when the Cherries headed to Charlton Athletic.

And after beating the Addicks 3-0, Elphick and his teammates celebrated wildly as news filtered through that a stoppage-time equaliser from Sheffield Wednesday's Atdhe Nuhiu against Watford ensured Eddie Howe's heroes would be crowned champions.

Elphick, who also skippered the Cherries to promotion from League One in 2012/13, joined the club's coaching staff in September 2021 after hanging up his boots, having made more than 400 appearances during a playing career spanning 16 years.

Recalling events from a glorious campaign for the Cherries, Elphick said: "We had finished the previous season very strongly and there was a bit of disappointment that we hadn't made the play-offs.

"In the summer, we signed some not only fantastic players but some really good characters who all just slotted in straight away and we had a great pre-season trip to Austria.

"I remember sitting down with a couple of the new lads one day and them telling me how good they thought training was.

"We knew if we could get off to a good start, we would have a chance of getting into the play-offs. There was a lot of anticipation and excitement.

"The manager would always plan things in pre-season and talk about our aims. We were well prepared and there was no reason why we couldn't knock on the door of the top six.

"We went to Huddersfield on the opening day and hit the ground running. Callum Wilson got his first goals for the club, and it all snowballed from there."

Although the Cherries won their first two games, three points from their next six matches left them in 15th place before goalkeeper Artur Boruc was drafted in on loan from Southampton.

A 14-match unbeaten run, which included 11 wins, saw the Cherries reach the end of the year in pole position, a point above Ipswich.

The sequence included a record-breaking 8-0 victory against Birmingham City at St Andrew's with Marc Pugh leading the way with a hat-trick.

"Artur Boruc was a big signing," said Elphick. "He was the final piece of the jigsaw. We had a great goalkeeper in Lee Camp at the time, but I just think Artur's experience and the confidence he gave us helped the team grow even more.

"I have always said the strength of our starting 11 was the lads behind it. You always knew there was someone waiting in the wings to take your position if you didn't perform.

"We knew how good the team behind was. When we played, we always trusted the process. Sometimes, the performance meant more than the result and that's what stood us in good stead because we always stuck to our principles."

Despite losing two of their first three games of 2015, back-to-back wins against Watford and Wigan saw them top the table in early February.

And their lengthy stay at the summit came to an end after honours had finished even when Derby visited Vitality Stadium on 10th February with Middlesbrough's win at Blackpool seeing them go top.

The Cherries regained pole position with ten games remaining but only on goal difference. They were one of four teams on 66 points with fifth-placed Norwich just a point behind.

The congested nature of the league saw the Cherries slip out of the automatic promotion places after drawing 1-1 at Cardiff before a clinical 3-0 win over Middlesbrough took them back to the top with seven games remaining.

And although an incident-packed 2-2 draw with Sheffield Wednesday threatened to spoil the party, the promotion dream finally became a reality when Bolton were beaten 3-0 at Vitality Stadium.

With the title on the line, there was still time for some late drama as Atdhe Nuhiu's late equaliser for Sheffield Wednesday at Watford ensured Howe's heroes would be crowned champions following their 3-0 win at Charlton.

"There were a few key games when I thought 'we can do this'. Brighton and Reading away and a great 1-1 draw at Ipswich where we came back to claim a point.

"We were really tough to play against during that period. We had all the different tools in our kit. We prided ourselves on playing out from the back, but we could also go direct if we needed to.

"We could grind out results and blow teams away as well. Our style of play was quick and attacking. Towards the end of the season, we showed so many different sides to our game.

"When we went to Charlton with the title on the line, the lessons of League One two years earlier when we didn't have a trophy to show off stood us in good stead.

"I don't care what anyone says, it's an amazing feeling getting promoted but there is no feeling like winning a title.

"It was a pleasure and a privilege to play in that game. We knew what was at stake and what we wanted to do. It was one of our best performances of the season.

"It was one of the most competitive Championship races ever to be run. When I compare the standard now to what it was then, it was much better.

"You only have to look at the Bolton team we played when we won promotion to see how strong it was. They had some great players and some big characters.

"I would pitch our team against any other which has won the Championship. I know some formidable teams are in there – Reading, Watford, Fulham, Aston Villa and Newcastle – but I still think we were the best.

"We had the balance and blend; we had the flair and the characters. We had everything and never held back. We never worried about going anywhere – it was always on our terms."

INVINCIBLE CHERRIES

Very rarely does a team go unbeaten throughout an entire league campaign.

Arsenal's men's side famously did it on their way to the 2003/04 Premier League title, while Rangers were not defeated in their 2020/2021 Scottish Premiership-winning season.

But AFC Bournemouth now have their own Invincibles to be proud of, in the form of their women's team during 2023/24.

HOW THE SEASON WENT

Under the management of boss Steve Cuss, the Cherries recorded a remarkable 19 victories from their 22 National League Division One South West games, drawing only three times in the process.

Cuss's troops recorded a positive goal difference of +91 as they entertained with goals galore throughout the entire unbeaten campaign.

Amazingly, they narrowly missed out on the league title and promotion from the fourth tier.

Exeter City totalled two more points following a draw against the Cherries on the final day of the season. Only one team gained promotion.

Regardless of that, Cuss insisted his team had plenty to be proud of, as they etched their names into the history books with a remarkable invincible campaign.

WHAT THE MANAGER SAID

Speaking after the final game of the league season, he said: "You set your stall out to be the best that you can be, and we've gone through the whole season and no one has been able to beat us.

"Exeter were worthy champions, but it's fine margins and I'm just so proud of the girls to be able to do that.

"To be able to have that ability to go through any league and not get beaten, it takes an incredible team to do that.

"They deserve an enormous amount of credit for that."

He added: "We've got to digest this and keep moving forward.

"That's what we want to do with the women's team. We've moved it forward year on year.

"We got closer this year. We've got to try and regroup, go again next year and maybe use this to spur us on a little bit."

FINISHING ON A HIGH

After narrowly missing out on the league title, Cuss's side did get a reward for their fine season, having won the Adopt South Women's Hampshire Senior Cup for the second year in a row.

Goals from Kenni Thompson, Lucy Cooper and Erin Bloomfield ensured AFC Bournemouth beat Southampton under-21s 3-1 in the final at Aldershot's EBB Stadium.

Striker Cooper finished with 22 goals for the season in all competitions, with Gemma McGuinness (19) and Bloomfield (16) also among the side's top scorers.

Midfielder Molly Barron-Clark was voted the team's player of the season, having registered 23 assists and scored 11 goals herself.

A DAY IN THE LIFE
ANTOINE SEMENYO

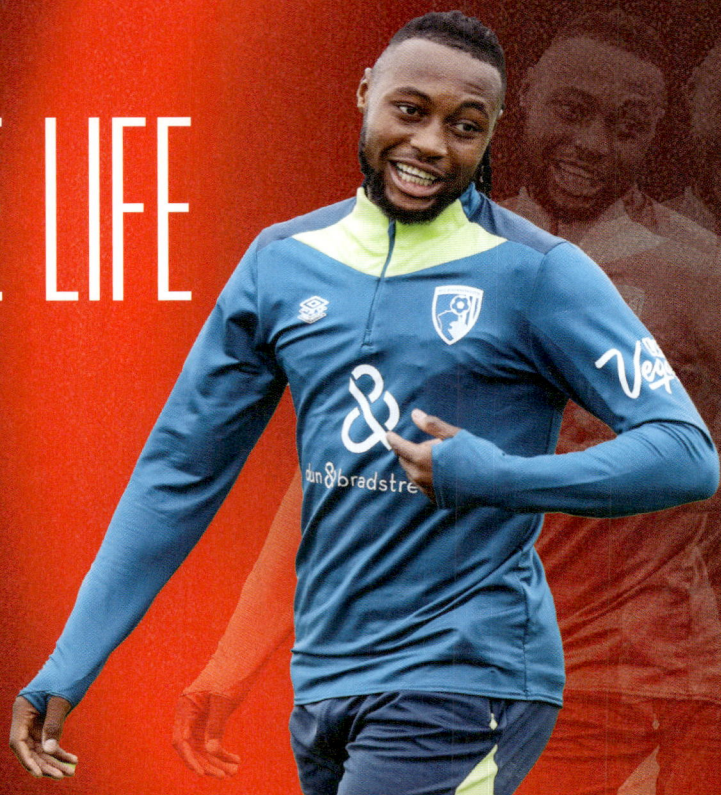

With around eight billion people on the planet, one 24-hour period can be experienced in vastly different ways. That can depend on the country you live in, the school you go to, your job or even vary between which team you play for at AFC Bournemouth. So here, first-team player Antoine Semenyo sheds a little light on what an average day in his life looks like...

7.30AM

Every day as a footballer is different depending on the training schedule, if we're travelling or playing a match but generally, I get up at 7.30am every morning.

I always start the day with a little prayer and thank God for protecting me through my sleep and blessing me with a new day!

Then, I check on the dog, make sure he's alright, feed him and take him out for a walk briefly.

8.40AM

After all that, it's time to set off and get to the training ground.

9AM

I'll usually arrive around 9am and get myself in, get changed and meet the boys because everyone's in for a new day.

We'll then go up to breakfast together and what I'm having there really depends on different things!

Some days I'm an omelette with toast man, some days I'd say I'm a porridge and toast with jam man, it just depends how I'm feeling on the day.

2.30PM

This is generally around the time we'll be leaving the training ground and I'll be getting home for somewhere around 3pm.

6PM

In the evening we'll generally have our dinner at home and try to get in as many of the food groups in as we do at lunch time.

What I do with the rest of my evening varies but I'll generally read the Bible and make some notes; I do that most evenings.

If not, I'll maybe watch Love Island!

10AM

We then have activation, which are exercises to get the legs ready for a tough session.

10.30AM

We're warmed up and getting out onto the pitches by this time, and from then we'll train for an hour or two.

That's always hard work and intense!

We've got good quality boys, and everyone's trying to impress and cause havoc! That's to show the head coach we want to be in the team; we're all trying to prove ourselves.

It's always good quality, so that's tough all round.

12.30PM

After training, it's lunch time and what that is depends on what's on offer!

I try to have carbohydrates, a lot of chicken and red meat, with lots of vegetables and starch.

What we have varies and it depends on what the chefs have made for lunch.

1.30PM

Depending on what the schedule is looking like, around now we'll have time in the gym, treatment or other work.

Potentially some media requirements, too! That could be interviews, photoshoots, anything really.

10-11PM

I'll get myself to bed around this time so I'm ready to go again for the same thing again in the morning.

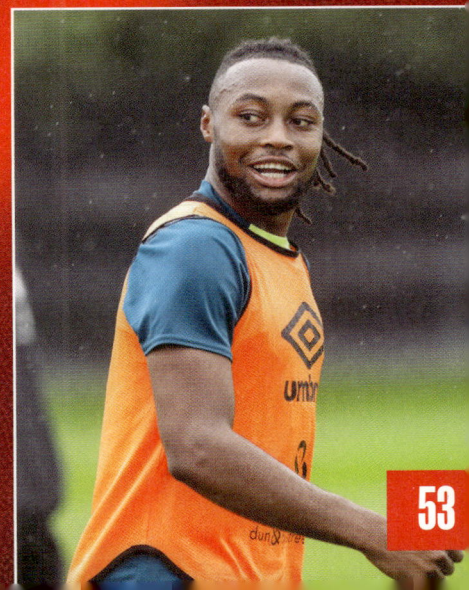

53

MAZE

CAN YOU GUIDE MARCUS TAVERNIER TO HIS BOOTS?

Marcus has a big game at Vitality Stadium, but he needs to locate his boots before he can play! Can you help him navigate through the maze to collect his boots?!

GO TO P62-63 FOR THE ANSWERS

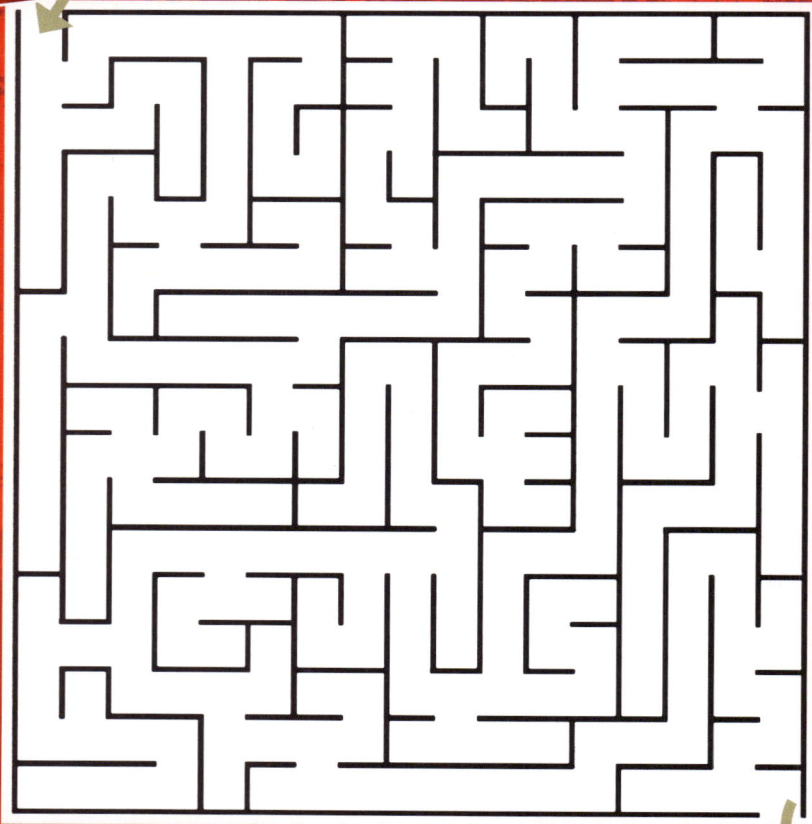

ANAGRAMS!

GO TO P62-63 FOR THE ANSWERS

Can you work out which Cherries heroes have had their names mixed up below?!

NOISE SCREAMS

CHEER FELT VETS

MADLY RATES

HONOUR SPACE

EASY NOMINEE NOT

WHO AM I?

GO TO P62-63 FOR THE ANSWERS

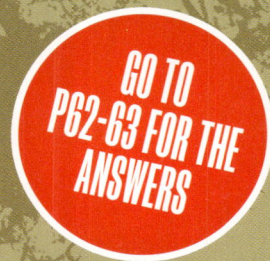

Take a look at the clues below and try to work out which Cherries star we're talking about. Give yourself a point for each one you get correct!

PLAYER 1:

- I started my career at Spurs
- I've been with the Cherries for over ten years
- I've won two promotions to the Premier League with AFC Bournemouth
- I'm the vice-captain of the team

ANSWER

PLAYER 2:

- I'm a centre-back
- I played 37 out of 38 Premier League games last season
- My first Cherries goal came in the 4-3 win over Luton
- I played at Euro 2024

ANSWER

PLAYER 3:

- I signed permanently for the club in 2024
- I joined the Cherries from Leeds
- My best friend in the squad in Marcos Senesi
- I come from Colombia

ANSWER

WORDSEARCH

GO TO P62-63 FOR THE ANSWERS

There are so many different words that we associate with AFC Bournemouth, but can you find them in the wordsearch?

S	X	R	I	P	F	A	H	L	V	V	Z	E	K	J	E	V	X	K	B
F	B	N	A	D	D	A	D	O	E	D	T	G	T	R	Y	M	J	A	K
G	R	V	S	B	T	Y	X	W	A	B	Q	L	D	A	S	G	R	R	K
Z	J	M	E	N	A	B	Q	O	L	Q	V	Q	Q	F	T	V	P	Y	V
S	Z	J	I	M	S	K	C	N	F	V	I	W	X	E	H	F	C	T	Y
Y	P	S	R	K	V	I	T	A	L	I	T	Y	S	T	A	D	I	U	M
T	R	P	R	E	M	I	E	R	L	E	A	G	U	E	I	E	P	X	O
F	E	T	E	W	R	O	P	L	A	K	E	I	K	P	Q	W	Q	C	G
L	N	A	H	O	H	X	L	H	Z	G	N	E	Q	A	D	H	B	E	O
Q	A	G	C	P	R	L	G	N	W	O	V	V	T	K	Y	T	H	H	W
O	J	U	E	K	A	H	W	H	D	M	Z	T	L	V	O	S	S	M	O
G	P	O	H	B	L	X	O	N	E	B	M	O	C	S	O	B	P	I	L
E	U	U	T	Q	W	Y	A	W	U	E	W	L	X	Y	S	S	Q	C	R
L	C	O	P	K	E	O	D	L	M	N	O	S	Z	K	M	A	U	K	V
G	O	O	U	Y	P	U	V	X	B	J	Y	P	B	I	S	V	I	J	F
F	X	L	B	A	N	G	I	R	F	E	H	Z	J	O	H	L	N	L	Y
D	H	A	E	Q	N	T	W	K	F	E	O	A	P	J	W	V	A	T	K
D	X	L	K	P	W	X	N	Z	F	M	N	P	O	F	L	L	Y	O	Y
U	L	E	Z	T	C	H	W	N	H	O	C	X	K	M	Q	K	D	T	G
A	A	O	B	V	J	R	V	C	X	X	R	K	R	I	V	V	B	S	O

Andoni

Boscombe

Football

Goals

Paella

Premier League

Up the Cherries

Vitality Stadium

LET'S GET QUIZZING!

WORD FIT

GO TO P62-63 FOR THE ANSWERS

Can you help place the names of players in our women's team in the grid below?!

Barron Clark   Hillier   Smith

Bleazard   James   Treweek

Cooper   Jones

Cuss   McGuinness

58

TRUE OR FALSE!

There's plenty to know about our head coach, Andoni Iraola! But it's time to test out your knowledge... Can you pick out which three facts are true and which two are false?

1. Andoni Iraola played in the Champions League.

ANSWER

2. He managed Spanish side Mirandés to the Copa del Rey final.

ANSWER

3. He was the first-ever Bournemouth head coach to oversee a win at Old Trafford.

ANSWER

4. While managing Rayo Vallecano, his side beat both Barcelona and Real Madrid in the same season.

ANSWER

5. Andoni Iraola's first management job came in Switzerland.

ANSWER

BONUS QUESTION:
6. True or false... Andoni Iraola won the Premier League Manager of the Month award in March 2024?!

ANSWER

GO TO P62-63 FOR THE ANSWERS

LET'S GET QUIZZING!

2014/15 QUIZ

It is ten years in April since our first-ever promotion to the Premier League, so we're looking back at that season. How many questions can you get right?!

GO TO P62-63 FOR THE ANSWERS

1. Which team did we beat 8-0 away from home?

ANSWER

2. Who was our top scorer that season?

ANSWER

3. Fill in the blank from an iconic bit of commentary: "_____, that'll do it!"

ANSWER

4. Who did we play on the last day of the season to win the title?

ANSWER

5. True or false: We ended up with a goal difference of over 50?

ANSWER

6. Which Cherries legend wore the number 8 shirt?

ANSWER

7. Who was our captain?

ANSWER

8. Which team did we beat 4-0 on the opening day?

ANSWER

9. How many points did we finish on – 80, 85 or 90?

ANSWER

10. Who was our South African number 9 that season?

ANSWER

NUMBER GAME!

How well do you know our squad numbers? Do the maths below and see which Cherries player you end up with...

GO TO P62-63 FOR THE ANSWERS

Ryan Christie's number (10) + Marcos Senesi's number (5) =

ANSWER

Illia Zabarnyi's number (27) - Milos Kerkez's number (3) =

ANSWER

Max Aarons' number (37) - Enes Ünal's number (26) =

ANSWER

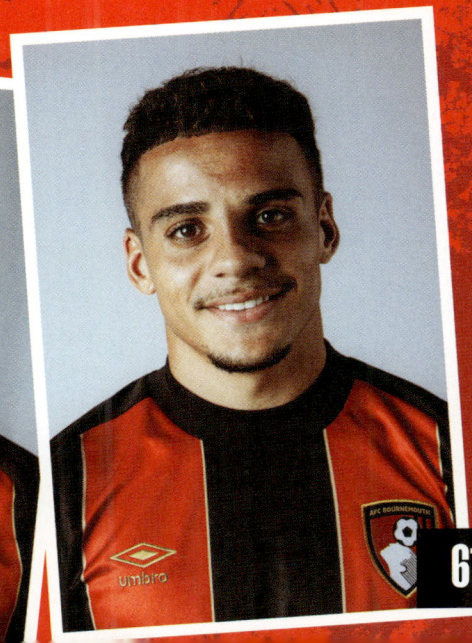

QUIZ ANSWERS

PAGE 54: MAZE

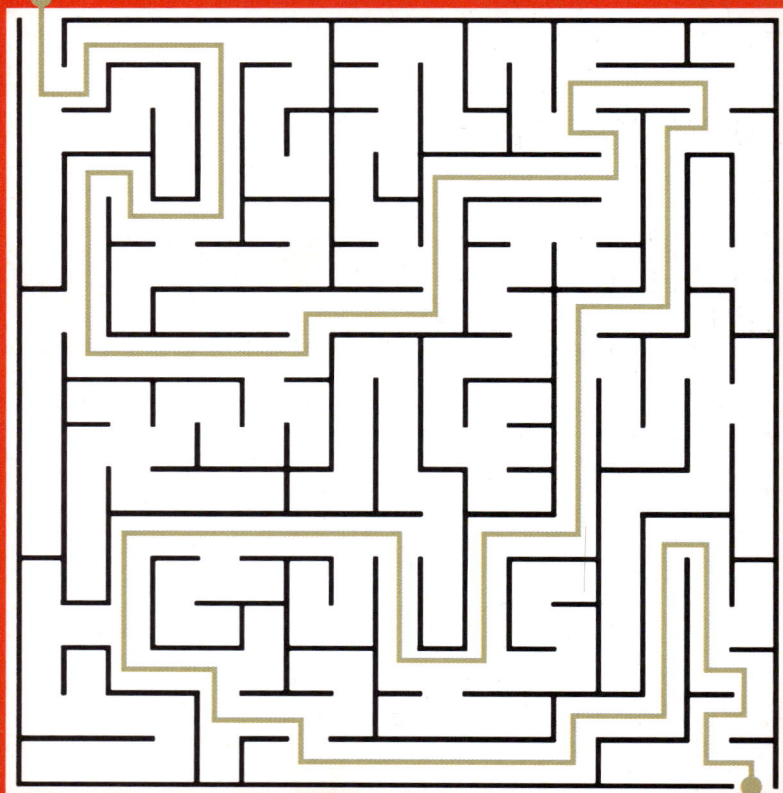

PAGE 55: ANAGRAMS!

NOISE SCREAMS
(MARCOS SENESI)

CHEER FELT VETS
(STEVE FLETCHER)

MADLY RATES
(TYLER ADAMS)

HONOUR SPACE
(SHAUN COOPER)

EASY NOMINEE NOT
(ANTOINE SEMENYO)

PAGE 56: WHO AM I?

Player 1: Adam Smith

Player 2: Illia Zabarnyi

Player 3: Luis Sinisterra

PAGE 59: TRUE OR FALSE!

1. True.
2. False, they got to the semi-finals.
3. True.
4. True.
5. False, it was Cyprus.

Bonus question: True.

PAGE 60: 2014/15 QUIZ

1. Birmingham City
2. Callum Wilson (23 in all competitions)
3. "Pugh, that'll do it!"
4. Charlton Athletic
5. True, it was +53!
6. Harry Arter
7. Tommy Elphick
8. Huddersfield Town
9. 90
10. Tokelo Rantie